How To Cook Healthy Recipes

A Beginner's Guide To Kitchen Basics For Healthy, Natural Meals At Home

Patrick Barrett

www.BarrettBooks.com

Copyright © 2012 Patrick Barrett

All rights reserved.

ISBN-10: 1480230030
ISBN-13: 978-1480230033

CONTENTS

Introduction	1
Basic Nutrition	6
Tools Of The Trade	13
One Step Farther	20
Basic Ingredients	24
Basic Techniques	30
Components Of A Meal	42
Making Cooking Convenient	46
Trial And Error	50
Recipes	53
Broiled Steak	55
Broiled Fish	57
Roasted Chicken	59
Roast Pork	61
Pan-Fried Fish	63
Pan-Fried Pork Chop	65
Simple Chili	67
Fried Egg	70
Sautéed Vegetables	72

Steamed Vegetables	74
Basic Beans	76
Simple Vegetable Soup	78
Basic Salad	80
Quinoa	82
Yogurt Dressing	84
Simple Gravy	85
Guacamole	87
Lemonade	90
Orange Juice	92
Sweet Green Tea	94
Breakfast Smoothie	97
Chocolate Milk	99
Leafy Fruit Smoothie	101
How To Find A Healthy Recipe Online	104
How To Make Stock	110
Seasoning	115
Connect With Me	117
Conclusion	119
Books By Patrick Barrett	122
About The Author	123

"You learn to cook so that you don't have to be a slave to recipes. You get what's in season and you know what to do with it."

-Julia Child, world-famous chef and TV cooking pioneer

Other Books by Patrick Barrett:

Natural Exercise: Basic Bodyweight Training And Calisthenics For Strength And Weight-Loss

Advanced Bodyweight Exercises: An Intense Full Body Workout In A Home Or Gym

The Natural Diet: Simple Nutritional Advice For Optimal Health In The Modern World

How To Do A Handstand: From The Basic Exercises To The Free Standing Handstand Pushup

Hand And Forearm Exercises: Grip Strength Workout And Training Routine

Best Ab Exercises: Abdominal Workout Routine For Core Strength And A Flat Stomach

Easy Exercises: Simple Workout Routine For Busy People In The Office, At Home, Or On The Road

One Arm Pull Up: Bodyweight Training And Exercise Program For One Arm Pull Ups And Chin Ups

Disclaimer:

This book was not written or reviewed by a doctor, personal trainer, dietitian, or other licensed person. Always consult with your doctor before beginning any exercise routine or implementing any change in your diet or medication.

INTRODUCTION

Hi! My name is Patrick Barrett, and I'd like to start by thanking you for buying this book. I know that your time and money are valuable, so I will do my very best to provide you with useful information, and help you to build a better lifestyle through healthy, delicious food that you can cook yourself.

I love to cook food, and I love to eat food. While I have always loved eating (perhaps more than I should), I haven't always been able to cook. I didn't really start until my second year of college, and I remember being intimidated by the whole idea. I didn't want to do a bunch of work and then end up eating something that wasn't any good. Above all, I didn't want to burn or ruin something and waste it.

Well, living on your own changes things, and before long I started to try out a few simple dishes. It didn't always go smoothly, especially in the beginning, but before long I actually learned to make a few things pretty well.

Over the years I've gotten much more comfortable in the kitchen, and I've even come up with a few recipes of my own—but the most important thing was always just getting over that initial fear, being willing to test some things out, and being okay with having a few meals that weren't exactly perfect while I was still getting used to the whole thing.

It's great to be able to cook your own food. When some of your favorite foods are dishes that you know how to make, you can have delicious meals any night you want. While I still love to eat in restaurants, I've gotten to the point where I actually prefer my own version of many meals to their restaurant equivalents.

However, there's another important reason that you need to learn to cook for yourself, and that's really the main reason that I decided to write this book. People who don't or can't cook for themselves end up eating prepared meals from restaurants or grocery stores. In today's world, those meals are more often than not loaded with industrial additives, artificial flavorings, preservatives, multiple variants of MSG, petroleum-based colorings, and who knows what else.

This doesn't just mean ready-to-eat meals, it also includes 'convenient' foods that come pre-seasoned and almost ready to go—basically anything that isn't made from scratch is likely to be a bad choice.

Because so much of the prepared food (or partially prepared food) available today is so loaded with various additives, one of the most important components of a healthy lifestyle is an abundance of foods prepared in the home.

In other words, if you want to be healthy, you need to know how to cook. The best way to cut all of that fake crap out of your diet, out of your body, and out of your life is to learn how to cook your own foods at home. You will be better for it, and your entire family (or whoever else eats with you) will be better for it too.

This book will teach you all the basics you need to know to cook your own food. You'll learn about the fundamental kitchen tools you'll need, and we'll also take a helpful look at some of the most common ingredients you'll use on a daily basis. We'll go over beginner cooking techniques, how to build a healthy meal, and how to embrace trial and error as you learn to cook.

We'll talk about what you need to avoid when you cook, how to season food, and how to make your own stock (this is important both for health reasons and for flavor). And, of course, we'll take a look at a full set of basic, highly-customizable recipes that will put you well on your way to a lifetime of healthy, delicious, home-cooked meals.

In perhaps the most useful section in this book, we'll talk about how to find recipes on your own, and how to change unhealthy recipes by eliminating unnatural ingredients and substituting healthier ones. Since the ingredients we're switching out are typically "fake," shortcut-versions of the real thing, the adjusted recipes will actually tend to taste better, in addition to being healthier.

One more thing—a big reason people don't cook their own food at home is that it is less convenient. To some extent that is unavoidable; after all, doing something yourself always takes more time than just having someone else do it. However, we can certainly make decisions that make cooking for yourself as convenient as possible without giving up the benefits that go along with it. For that reason, sometimes I'll recommend an option that's just barely less than ideal if it means you do a whole lot less work.

For example, I might recommend that you eat canned beans with no additives in them as opposed to buying dry beans, soaking them for hours and then cooking them for an additional hour. The canned beans require maybe 2% of the effort and deliver 95% of the benefits. I don't know about you, but canned beans sound like the way to go to me—after all, there's no point in designing an ideal way to cook and eat food if no one is going to stick to it because it's such a pain.

So, while there will always be purists who argue that there is some even better way to purchase or prepare certain foods—and they may well be right—we will focus on the very best option that is actually feasible in the real world for most people. You can certainly always feel free to go that extra step, or two, or ten, if that's what you want to do, but most people will get the most benefit out of the option that fits more easily into their lives.

One more thing—posting reviews on Amazon is a huge deal for authors like me. Many people who read and enjoy a book never think to leave a good review, even if they're very happy with it.

If you find this book to be helpful, it would be awesome if you could consider leaving even a short positive review.

Okay! Let's get started.

Books by Patrick Barrett:

Natural Exercise: Basic Bodyweight Training And Calisthenics For Strength And Weight-Loss

Advanced Bodyweight Exercises: An Intense Full Body Workout In A Home Or Gym

The Natural Diet: Simple Nutritional Advice For Optimal Health In The Modern World

How To Do A Handstand: From The Basic Exercises To The Free Standing Handstand Pushup

Hand And Forearm Exercises: Grip Strength Workout And Training Routine

Best Ab Exercises: Abdominal Workout Routine For Core Strength And A Flat Stomach

Easy Exercises: Simple Workout Routine For Busy People In The Office, At Home, Or On The Road

One Arm Pull Up: Bodyweight Training And Exercise Program For One Arm Pull Ups And Chin Ups

BASIC NUTRITION

Well, the point of this whole endeavor is for you to learn to make delicious meals that are healthy, so it makes sense to talk about nutrition for a little while before we start talking about how to cook.

The most important advantage of home-cooked meals that we will focus on time and again is the absence of unnecessary chemicals and additives in meals you make at home compared to prepared foods you can get elsewhere. Prepared stuff you find at grocery stores is full of extra ingredients whose purpose is to extend shelf-life and artificially cram in flavor and color in the most cost-effective way. That's bad news for your body.

However, just as important as what you are not eating (all those additives) is what you actually are eating. In other words, avoiding all that stuff is good, but you still want to make sure that what you do cook is good for you. That means we need to talk about what's good for you, so that we're both on the same page.

I discuss this in much more detail in my book The Natural Diet, but let's do a quick run-through.

Learning about nutrition is extremely confusing in the modern world, but knowing what's good for you is actually very simple. The biggest problem we face as a society when it comes to eating healthy is that we overthink it. All those health experts on TV, online, and in magazines need something to talk about every month, week, and day of the year, so they always find some new trend or theory that they want to tell you about so you will buy their magazine, or watch their show, or pay $59 every month for their supplement.

That means people are constantly inundated with more 'new' information about about the right way to eat healthy, and they're constantly trying to adjust accordingly. However, the obvious truth here is that the human body's nutritional needs don't change. Your body is not like a car or a phone or a computer; a new one doesn't come out every year with different specs and components. The human body has been essentially unchanged for millenia, and what the human body needs has been essentially unchanged as well. Once you know to shut out all the talking heads and stick to what makes sense, makes you feel good, and gets results, all of that will seem much, much simpler and easier.

Your body is something ancient living in a modern world. Its needs are ancient too. That means a good rule of thumb is only to eat foods that would have been available a century ago or more. Many of today's hyper-processed foods require a factory and tons of equipment to produce, and for the most part you want to avoid anything like that, and anything else that doesn't come directly out of the earth, the sea, or an animal.

What your body needs now are the same foods it has always needed. We'll take a look at more of those in turn throughout the book, but to sum it up we'll say that we're going to focus on a diet that features primarily fruits, vegetables, animal proteins, beans, dairy, eggs, and good fats (these are probably not what you expect), and avoids artificial additives, bad fats, and starches. Above all, we want to stick to a minimally processed diet as much as possible.

On that note, let's take a quick look at fat, protein, and carbohydrates in turn, so we're on the same page when it comes to the three main components of your diet.

Fat

Fat is a very important part of your diet and also of delicious food, and it is also probably one of the least understood parts of our diet. You need fat to be healthy, and the fats that are actually healthy are not the ones you frequently hear about from the mainstream experts.

Most people do most of their cooking with vegetable oil (which is actually soybean oil) and canola oil (which is actually rape oil). Let's talk briefly about how canola oil is produced.

The rapeseeds are ground up. This releases the oil from inside the shell, but the bits of shell are still clinging to the bits of oil. In order to separate the shell from the oil, hexane—a hydrocarbon and mild anesthetic found in gasoline and heavy-duty glues—is mixed in. That separates the shells from the oil, but then you're left with a mixture of oil and hexane.

Those are put into a centrifuge which removes most of the hexane, but not all of it. A bottle of canola oil you see on the shelf at a grocery store still contains a small percentage of hexane that they couldn't separate out.

Afterward, the fat smells awful, because it's rancid. You see, polyunsaturated fats (like those in rapeseeds) are very unstable, so once they come out of the shell and get exposed to light and heat and air, they start to break down. That means at this point in the process, the oil is decomposing and smells terrible.

To get rid of that smell, the oil is blasted with superheated steam to burn off any rotten flavor or odor, which actually gets rid of any flavor or odor at all. That's why these oils don't taste or smell like anything.

So, what you're left with is an odorless, flavorless, decomposing oil that contains a little bit of hexane. This is not natural, and it's not what you want in your kitchen or in your body. Soybean oil (sold as vegetable oil) goes through a similar process.

Here are some fats that are good—that you want to cook with—listed in order of increasing smoke point (the temperature at which they start to smoke; you want to keep them below this temperature):

- Butter
- Coconut Oil
- Olive Oil
- Peanut Oil

These are fats that people have eaten for centuries. Unlike vegetable oil and canola oil, they actually have an odor and flavor, because they aren't decomposing industrial products. Also, although they are made in factories today, they don't require a factory for production and have been made by people for a long, long time. Stick with healthy, minimally processed fats like these when you cook.

Protein

Just as you need fat, your body of course needs protein. We want to keep up the theme of eating natural, minimally processed foods to get your protein, so we will talk mostly about eating animal proteins from a variety of sources, including beef, fish, pork, and chicken, as well as eggs and dairy products. You want them to be as close to their natural state as possible, so buy meat unseasoned and stick to dairy products without any artificial ingredients.

Great non-animal sources of protein include beans and lentils. We will cover the basics for all of these later in the book so you will have a full range to choose from.

Carbohydrates

Many people consume a high proportion of the carbohydrates in their diets from wheat sources, such as bread and pasta. Such foods tend to be highly processed and tend not to contain much nutrition, which can lead to weight gain and poor health. They also contain gluten, a protein which many people have varying degrees of sensitivity to—many are not even aware of it. Symptoms of this sensitivity can include bloating, diarrhea, and intestinal discomfort, as well as headaches and lethargy.

There are a lot of reasons to limit or eliminate wheat products in your diet: they tend to have little nutritional value, they can be associated with unpleasant side effects for many people, and most importantly, there are many other carbohydrate options that are simply much healthier.

For all of these reasons, we will minimize or eliminate wheat-containing foods, and in this book we will focus on getting carbohydrates from fresh fruit and a variety of vegetable dishes, as well as from the beans and lentils we just talked about in the protein section. There are also some non-wheat grains, like quinoa, which are healthier sources of carbohydrates than wheat is, and which provide a measure of protein as well.

****

If you'd like a more detailed explanation of all of this, be sure to take a look at my book The Natural Diet. Otherwise, this covers everything you need to know for the purposes of this book.

One more thing to bear in mind—even if you don't agree 100% with my views on nutrition, you can still find a lot of value in this book. For example, if you're a vegetarian, you obviously will not be getting any protein from meat sources. However, there are a lot of meatless recipes in this book, and more importantly you will learn a lot about the basics behind cooking your own food while avoiding those undesirable additives. Regardless of what you're cooking, you can still apply those same basic ideas so that you avoid additives no matter what dietary principles you subscribe to.

Okay! Now that we're on the same page with nutrition, let's continue by talking about the specific tools you will be using in your kitchen on a daily basis.

TOOLS OF THE TRADE

Once you know how to cook, you've developed a skill that you will probably use most of the days of your life. If you're going to spend that much time doing something, you need to learn a little more about the best kinds of equipment to use.

This information will help to ensure that you stick to healthy cooking by avoiding some of the aggravation caused by sub-par tools. You'll also learn some very important facts about non-stick cooking surfaces. Let's get to it.

Knife

Your knife might be the single most important tool in your kitchen. Chopping vegetables and cutting meat are two very simple activities, but they can both become very difficult and discouraging when the knife you are using is inadequate. Chopping an onion or a pepper or a tomato with a dull knife is a huge pain, and a great way to make yourself never want to cook again. A lot of cooking is chopping, so this is important.

Although there are many different types of knives designed for a variety of specific tasks, 95% of regular people can satisfy 95% of their regular kitchen needs with a simple, standard chef's knife. They can run into the many hundreds of dollars, but you should be able to get by with one that costs less than $20, and you should be able to be happy with one that costs less than $50.

If you go for a knife that costs less than $20, it will probably be a stamped blade. That means the shape of the blade is cut out of a piece of flat steel (like a cookie-cutter, sort of) and the blade itself will be uniformly flat and shapeless with a sharpened edge. These can be sharpened to a tolerable level, but they will dull relatively quickly (maybe in a week to a month, depending on frequency and type of use). If you don't want to spend more and you don't mind sharpening the blade more often (we'll talk about sharpening in a minute), this can be perfectly adequate. Here's a picture of a knife with a stamped blade:

A knife more in the $50 range will probably have a forged blade. A forged blade is made so that the blade itself has a little bit more shape and heft to it, usually a little thicker toward the back and thinner closer to the sharpened edge. Since the blade has been forged, it is much stronger. It will last longer and hold its edge longer. This is definitely the better type of knife to buy, although, again, a stamped blade can be fine. Here's a picture of a knife with a forged blade:

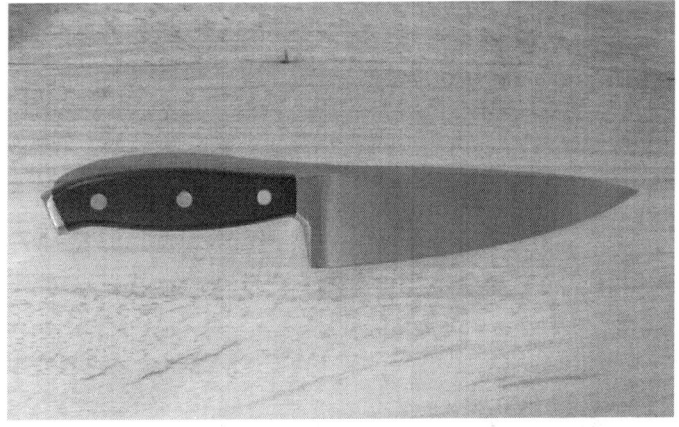

As far as sharpening the knife, a chef's knife connoisseur will insist that you use a whetstone, and you probably should, especially if you spend a ton of money on a really nice knife, or if you're hoping the knife will be a family heirloom someday. However, if you just want a knife that does what it's supposed to do without labor-intensive upkeep, you can just use a standard two-stage knife sharpener like the one pictured here:

Follow the instructions that come with your particular sharpener, and be sure to clean your knife thoroughly afterward. Using this thing every couple of weeks when you notice the blade dulling a little takes about five minutes, and it ensures that when you cook you can focus on what you're actually trying to make, instead of chasing a tomato slice all around the cutting board with your knife because the blade won't actually cut into it.

One quick note: once you buy a real chef's knife (even the $20 one), don't wash it in the dishwasher. All that banging around will dull the blade pretty quickly. Always wash your chef's knife by hand after use, then dry it and put it away.

One more quick note: don't buy a serrated chef's knife. Serrated knives tear instead of slicing, and the difference can mean a lot more aggravation in the kitchen. They tend to be a lot cheaper, but that's because they are easier to make and not as good. Avoid them.

Cutting Board

Well, if your knife is important, you're obviously going to need something to do all of that cutting on. Getting a good cutting board is important for two reasons: (1) it helps take care of your knife, and (2) it ensures food safety.

Never use a glass or marble cutting board with your chef's knife. You don't want a surface that is that hard, because it will ruin the edge of your knife. Don't use your chef's knife on this type of cutting board.

The two main types of cutting board left are wood and plastic. Some people are die-hard wood cutting board users, and some will only use plastic, but the bottom line is that either is fine as long as you care for them properly. Wood is probably a little better but takes more work to care for, plastic is maybe not quite as good but has much easier upkeep. I have a couple of each and I use them all.

Both are fine for your knife because they are not so rigid that they will ruin your blade; that's not really an issue with wood or plastic cutting boards. The main difference to consider between the two has to do with bacteria. When you use your knife on either surface, you end up creating small grooves in the cutting board. Those grooves can hold both bacteria from cutting contaminated meats (raw chicken or pork is typically the biggest culprit here), and water from the cleaning process that doesn't quite get dried off.

That combination means your cutting board, if not properly cared for, can harbor bacteria which can make you sick. Some people prefer wood because, as it will absorb some water, it dries faster, creating a less friendly environment for bacteria, and cutting food on wood cannot result in tiny bits of plastic getting into your food. Others prefer plastic because it doesn't crack or warp like wooden boards often do, and it can go in the dishwasher without being ruined.

The bottom line is that if you thoroughly wash either a plastic or wooden cutting board and thoroughly dry afterward, you shouldn't run into any bacteria problems. I tend to use plastic most of the time, and especially when I need to cut raw chicken, because I like that I can put it into the dishwasher to be sanitized afterward. Also, wood cutting boards are more high maintenance and tend to warp and crack before too long unless you are meticulous about quickly drying them after each washing and rubbing them down with food-grade oil once a month or so.

Also, you probably want to replace your cutting boards (wood or plastic) when they get worn out, maybe a few times a year. After a lot of use they develop a lot of grooves that get harder and harder to clean, so it can be best just to start fresh with a new one.

Skillet

This is extremely important. Do not cook with typical 'non-stick' cookware. The process of creating that non-stick surface involves a variety of chemicals that are best avoided, and there are several potential health problems that range from the fumes that may be released from pans at higher cooking temperatures to the risk of ingesting small bits of the non-stick coating as the pan is used more and more and the coating flakes off.

Although numerous studies on both sides of the issue have shown a variety of effects of cooking with non-stick surfaces that range from negative to neutral, there is an easy solution that avoids the whole question with a time-tested method: cooking with either enameled cast iron or stainless steel.

A major 'benefit' people cite with non-stick pans is that you can cook with little or no fat in the pan and food won't stick, even at higher temperatures. As you'll see, we will be cooking with fat anyway (because it's healthy and delicious) and we typically don't even want to cook at higher temperatures in the first place.

Stainless steels pots and pans can work great; you'll just want to make sure to use some fat in the pan when you're sautéing something to avoid sticking, and make sure you hand wash with warm, soapy water afterward.

Enameled cast iron is another great option. As with the stainless steel, cook with some fat when sautéing, and hand wash with warm soapy water after use. Also, with cast iron you want to put the skillet on a stove and allow it to heat for maybe two or three minutes before putting anything in the skillet, and you never want to go higher than medium heat. Also, before washing, allow the pan to cool, or else you may cause the pan to warp or the coating to crack when you expose a hot pan to room-temperature water.

Of course, read any instructions that come with your particular pan, and be sure to follow their recommendations over mine if there's any contradiction.

You can also use regular cast iron without an enamel coating, but it will require a good deal more maintenance. Again, always read and follow the directions on any skillet or other cookware you decide to buy.

ONE STEP FARTHER

Okay, we've covered the basic tools. Now we'll talk about a few more things that can make life easier in the kitchen.

Remember that the two biggest factors that will keep you eating healthy and making food for yourself are taste and convenience. If there's a piece of equipment that can help you make delicious food more quickly and easily, you might want to think about getting it. These are some of my favorites, starting with the most practical.

Rice Cooker/Vegetable Steamer

There are lots of rice cookers and vegetable steamers out there. The one that I use is called the "Aroma ARC-838TC Digital Rice Cooker and Food Steamer." The name doesn't exactly roll off the tongue, but it does a great job. I've used it quite a bit and I've got no complaints.

I use this puppy several times a week. Making rice or quinoa is absurdly easy; just put in the water and the rice or quinoa, close the lid, and press "cook." That's it. It even automatically switches when it's done to keep the food warm for hours, and you can set a timer to delay the cooking, in case you want to get it ready earlier in the day and have it start later on.

It's just as easy to steam vegetables—simply check in the instruction manual to see how much water to use for a particular vegetable, put the water in the bottom and the vegetable in the little vegetable steamer basket that comes with it, and press "cook."

I have to say, if you like your steamed vegetables a little more on the crisp side, you might want to use less water than they recommend, but you'll get the hang of it the more you use it.

You can also use it to steam meat and seafood, although this is a function I haven't used too much.

Anyway, it's a staple in my kitchen, and if you're into making these types of foods, you should definitely consider it.

Citrus Juicer

My citrus juicer of choice is the "Tribest CS-1000 Citristar Citrus Juicer." I love this thing. The problem with most juicers is they aren't powerful enough, and they'll either stall out when you press too hard, or they don't get all the juice out, or both.

Also, many have an annoying and pointless feature where the reamer switches directions sometimes, which does not get out more juice and can make it harder to hold the fruit in place while it's being juiced.

This one is powerful enough to completely juice any citrus, but it's still not crazy expensive. At around $45, you might be tempted to buy one of the many $20 citrus juicers, but if you're actually going to get use out of it, I would recommend going with this one.

Also, when you consider that a decent traditional fruit juicer can cost hundreds of dollars, takes more time to clean up, and yields less juice for every piece of fruit when compared to a citrus juicer, the $45 or so starts to seem a lot more attractive.

Being able to have fresh fruit juice when you want it while keeping the work and cost to a minimum is awesome, and if it sounds good to you, then I would recommend you consider this juicer.

Blender

If you do a lot of blending, a good blender makes a world of difference. This piece of equipment is less necessary and more expensive than the last two, but it's something to consider if you start making a lot of smoothies—and you can also use it to make soups, dips, even your own peanut butter.

I've got a Blendtec blender, which I use at least once a day. I've had it for several years, and I love it.

Here's the bad news—new ones cost more than $400. Here's the better news: I got mine refurbished on eBay for less than half of that, and I've had no problems (except I did have to buy a replacement jar after a thousand uses, which is to be expected).

I can't recommend a certain seller, and I don't even know if the person who sold me mine is still active, but the point is that you look around at places like eBay, and you find somebody who has great feedback selling refurbished Blendtec blenders, it might be worth a shot.

I also know a few people who have the Ninja blender, at around $100, and although I have no personal experience with them, the people I know who have them seem to like them.

****

So, there you have it—3 more tools that get a lot of use in my kitchen, and that might have a home in yours too. These aren't strictly necessary, but if you think they would make it easier for you to prepare your own meals on a regular basis, then you should definitely consider getting them.

The biggest thing standing in between most people and healthy, in-home meals is convenience, so if any of these pieces of equipment make life a little easier for you, it's worth it.

BASIC INGREDIENTS

Now that we've covered some of the underlying ideas of the natural approach to cooking, as well as discussed what tools you'll need to perform in the kitchen, let's talk in a little detail about some of the ingredients you'll be using most often.

Sea Salt

Avoid ordinary table salt. Instead, always use sea salt. Sea salt contains a natural mix of minerals which are alkalizing to your body, instead of acidifying. You'll find that you don't need to use a ton of salt when cooking your own food anyway, but when you do use salt, always make it sea salt.

Onions

You'll be cooking and eating a lot of different vegetables, but onions get a special mention because of their versatility. Many, many recipes start with chopping and sautéing an onion, and onions can be used to create a whole range of flavors to be included in soups, sauces, stews, vegetable side dishes, meat dishes, and much more.

Spices

There are dozens of spices you can use, and once you get comfortable in the kitchen you'll probably regularly use around a half dozen to a dozen of them. Spices add a ton of flavor to your food, not to mention an assortment of minerals, antioxidants, and other good stuff. If you're new to cooking, don't be afraid of spices. Start with the basics, then get to know them one at a time as you try them in different dishes. We'll get into this more later, but for now I wanted to introduce them to you and make sure that you're not intimidated by them.

Wine

Wine can add amazing flavor to sautéed vegetables, pan-fried meats, soups, you name it. Like most ingredients, learning to cook with wine means just, well, starting to cook with wine. The big thing to remember with wine is to make sure that you use regular wine (not "cooking wine"), and that you cook off the alcohol taste. You'll get a sense of how to do this as we progress, and we'll discuss it in more detail later.

Soy Sauce

Although I do not recommend soy foods as a general rule, real, fermented soy sauce can be a great addition to a variety of meals.

There are two basic ways that companies make soy sauce. One of them involves fermentation, and takes some time. The other involves hydrolyzing protein, and is much quicker. Only use real, fermented soy sauce, not the hydrolyzed kind. The fermentation is an important part of the process which neutralizes a lot of bad things that are present in soybeans.

When you buy soy sauce (as when you buy anything that has an ingredient list), check the ingredients. Find a brand that is actually fermented and does not contain anything "hydrolyzed," or anything else hard to pronounce. Every ingredient on the list should be something you recognize, and it should basically be some combination of water, wheat, soybeans, and salt. Avoid the words "hydrolyzed" and "benzoate" and any other unusual words. You might need to go organic to satisfy this requirement; it's worth the extra dollar or two.

Be sure to use only soy sauce that meets this standard, and nothing else. It tastes better and is much better for you.

Lemon

Lemon and lime are two delicious citrus flavors used in a lot of dishes, especially those involving seafood. Everybody has different tastes, but some of you will end up using these ingredients quite a bit. Avoid the lemon or lime juice that most stores sell in bottles at room temperature. These juices, even ones that say "100% Lemon Juice" right on the bottle, contain preservatives that you want to avoid.

You have two viable options when it comes to adding lemon to your dishes. One is to keep lemons on hand, which is ideal. Fresh is always best, both for flavor and for nutrition.

However, a less expensive and more convenient—but still viable—option is frozen lemon juice. Always check the ingredient list when you first buy it to make sure, but frozen lemon juice should contain no additives. You should be able to find this in your grocery store near the juice concentrates. I've seen it as a small bottle of lemon juice inside of a small box (for some reason).

This lemon juice actually is 100% lemon juice with no preservatives (the fact that it is immediately frozen means they don't have to use preservatives), and once you thaw it, it stays good for about 8 weeks. I always keeps some of this on hand as a decent alternative to fresh lemon juice that still has no preservatives.

Balsamic Vinegar

Balsamic vinegar is another great ingredient you can add to meats and vegetables in a variety of situations. The flavor can be quite strong, so as with anything else, you should start small, experiment, and find out how you like to use it.

Garlic

Garlic is delicious, and it's good for you. It has various health benefits attributed to it, including antiviral, antibacterial, anti-heart disease, and anti-cancer properties. As always, fresh garlic is best, and you'll want to keep some on hand. You can buy garlic already peeled, but it tends to go bad much more quickly than unpeeled garlic. Raw garlic is incredibly pungent, and like most foods the intensity of its flavor decreases, and the flavor itself changes, the more it is cooked.

Garlic powder does not quite have the same flavor and health benefits as fresh garlic, but it is still good to have on hand, and it is something you will probably use a lot for its combination of flavor and convenience.

Canned or Frozen Vegetables

Canned vegetables are great to have on hand—provided you check out the ingredients. Choose vegetables and brands that put nothing more than water, salt, and the vegetables themselves into the cans (sometimes you will see calcium chloride in there; this isn't the end of the world, but if there's an option without it, then choose that). As with the soy sauce, you may need to go organic with some vegetables to satisfy this requirement.

After you buy the vegetables a couple of times you'll start to remember which brands of which vegetables don't have the extra crap in them, but for the first couple of times you will need to look at the ingredients of the things you buy. It doesn't take long to sort out the good from the bad, and it is well worth it.

You can also buy frozen vegetables, of course, provided their ingredient lists meet the same standard, but they are a little less convenient to store, and can be a pain if dinner rolls around and you've forgotten to thaw them. On the other hand, frozen vegetables are less likely to have preservatives and other additives, since they're frozen.

And, of course, fresh vegetables are wonderful, and are the best option for both flavor and health, but they are a little more expensive and a little less convenient. The most important thing with vegetables like this (especially if you're going to cook them anyway) is the lack of preservatives and chemicals. After that, you can pick whichever choice from canned, frozen, or fresh is most practical for you.

BASIC TECHNIQUES

If you're going to learn how to cook, you'll need to be familiar with a few basic techniques. We'll take a look at them in this chapter, but before we do, let's address a related issue.

If you already cook a little bit (or a lot), you'll probably be familiar with most of these skills. If not, though, some of this might seem intimidating.

I remember how I felt before I learned to cook for myself —the idea of creating a meal was daunting because I didn't want to ruin anything. I wanted to be able to know exactly how much of what went where, and I was worried that if I didn't know every part of how it was supposed to work then it would be a disaster.

It was never a disaster, but there were times in the beginning when things didn't exactly go as planned. If you're learning to do some of these things for the first time, you must accept the fact that the first couple of times you try to cook anything, it's probably not going to come out quite right—because you forgot to do something, because you aren't used to your stove yet, because you don't know how to season things to your own personal tastes, or for a variety of other reasons.

But those first couple of times are a crucial part of the learning process—you'll never be able to read any number of books or watch any number of videos and nail it on your very first try. Any time you read about a technique or a recipe in this book, you'll get a good idea of what you need to do, but you won't really know how to do it until you've actually done it a couple of times in real life.

Bear that in mind as you read the rest of this book—you're not going to come away from it knowing exactly how to do all of these things, but you will come away knowing enough so that you can go into your kitchen and learn them in real life, which is of course what counts.

If you go along and you read something and think "well, I'm not exactly sure how that's going to look," or "how will I know when it's done?" or something along those lines, just relax. I'll provide all the information I can, but some of those things you just can't be certain about until you get in there and try them, and at that point you can pick them up pretty quickly.

So if you come away from this book feeling less than certain about some of the concepts, that's totally fine. Once you spend a little time in the kitchen trying things out, you will quickly feel better.

Having said all of that, some of these ideas are pretty simple and won't be much of an issue anyway—but for the ones that are less clear-cut, don't worry.

Let's take a look:

Chopping

One thing you will most likely do a lot of is chopping. Of course, this is where the knife and the cutting board we discussed earlier will come into play.

There are two primary concerns to bear in mind when you are chopping. The first is safety.

Your chef's knife is sharp, and it can cut through you just as easily as it can cut through your food. Always be extremely careful when you chop anything, no matter how many times you've done it—but be especially careful if you aren't used to being in the kitchen, or to cutting things up, or to using a knife that's actually sharp.

The second concern, after safety, is how well you actually cut up what you're cutting. I find that that means chopping the vegetable in as orderly a fashion as possible. Everyone has their own way that they like to cut things; in the pictures below you can see how I like to cut an onion:

First you see the whole onion, then with top and bottom chopped off, then with the skin peeled off, then cut in half down the middle and laid flat, then sliced top-to-bottom, then sliced left to right, always with the blade moving downward toward the cutting board.

I tend to like pieces to be on the small side when I cook them up, but you'll figure out what you like. Just try some different things, and above all be careful.

Sautéing

Sautéing something basically just means putting some oil or butter in a skillet, turning on the heat, then cooking something in the skillet. For our purposes, it's basically the same as pan-frying something.

You put the skillet on the stove, put the oil or butter in there and turn it up to around medium heat. Let the fat heat for a few minutes, until it's warm enough that it moves around like water when you tilt the pan in one direction or the other. Then, you put whatever you're sautéing into the pan, and move it around so it gets coated with the fat and heat. Season and cook to your liking.

Reducing

There is a lot of water involved in cooking. Usually, this isn't water that you add, it's water/liquid that cooks out of a vegetable (onion, green peppers, cabbage, etc.).

Sometimes, you end up with more water than you wanted. This isn't ideal, because more water usually means less taste. If you think about it, when someone says something tastes watered down, that's usually not a compliment.

However, many times a lot of the flavor in a dish is suspended in the liquid in the pan. It gets to be a mix of butter or oil, wine, juices from vegetables, spices, and so on. So you don't want to just pour it off because then you'll lose all the flavor.

It might sound confusing to say that the dish is watered down and also that the liquid is very flavorful—the point is that there is a lot of flavor floating in the liquid, but it can be too diluted by the water. If you can get the water out of there without taking out the other stuff, then you'll be left with a very flavorful, thicker liquid (basically a sauce).

That's where reducing comes in. When you're cooking something with too much water in it, you simply turn the heat up (usually to around medium or high-medium) until it's hot enough that the water starts to cook off, and leave the pan as steam. The water evaporates, but all the parts of the liquid with flavor stay behind, so you're left with a more concentrated version of the sauce/liquid in the pan.

Of course, you want to pay close attention while you do this, especially in the beginning, because you're turning the heat up and you don't want anything to burn if too much of the water cooks off and you're left with no liquid at all. Keep an eye on the pan, and be sure to keep things moving if the level of liquid gets very low so what you're cooking doesn't burn. Once you're happy with the amount of liquid left behind, turn the heat to low and either season further, or serve the dish according to what you're trying to make.

Steaming

One of the simplest ways to prepare food is just to steam it; typically this is done with vegetables, but you can really do it with almost anything if you want to. It's not incredibly flavorful on its own, but you can add butter or some simple sauce afterward.

Probably the two most common ways to steam food are with a steamer basket, or with a vegetable steamer/rice cooker. We'll look at both.

With a steamer basket, you fill a pot with enough water so that it just touches the bottom of the steamer basket. Here's what a steamer basket looks like, open and closed.

Bring the water to a boil, then put the food into the basket. Cover loosely (make sure a little of the steam can get out) until the food is cooked, then turn off the heat and carefully remove the basket.

The other option is to do it in a vegetable steamer. These are often also used as rice cookers, since they work in a similar way. A vegetable steamer is convenient because it's easier to use and accomplishes the same thing.

Every steamer can be a little different, and you should follow the instructions on yours, but basically it will consist of a basket suspended above some water in a pot. You will put the correct amount of water in the pot according to the instructions in the steamer, put the vegetables (or seafood, or whatever) in the basket, close the lid, and turn it on. Most steamers will turn off automatically, and many will even keep the food warm until it is served.

Broiling

You can broil almost anything, but I tend to reserve broiling for steaks and, to a lesser extent, fish.

To broil something, you will need an oven and a broiling pan. Basically, you'll put the meat or fish on the broiling pan, turn on the broiler, and put the pan into the oven, leaving the oven door just a little open. The top part of the food is cooked from above by the heat of the burner in the oven, and then you need to open the door, flip the meat or fish, and put it back into the oven (with the door slightly open) to cook the other side.

Those are the basics, but there are some finer points to consider here. First of all, you need to move the top rack of the oven high enough so that the food itself (not the pan, the food on top of it) is around four inches from the heat source in the top of the oven. If your rack can't go high enough to get it that close, move it as high as you can.

You will need to turn the broiler on high before you start broiling, and give it a few minutes (maybe 3 or so) to heat up, for best results.

Leave the meat in there for a few minutes, then flip to cook the other side until it is done to your liking.

This is another area where you will have to learn about your own tastes, and learn about your oven. If you can't get the rack close enough to the heat, it will obviously take some more time to cook. Also, not every broiler cooks at the same temperature, and even those that are supposed to be the same temperature can vary. Don't worry though—you'll start to learn these things very quickly once you actually do them.

If you're cooking steak, you will want to learn to time it to your desired degree of doneness. If you're cooking anything else, you will want to make sure to broil it until it's cooked through.

Roasting

You can roast chicken, pork, beef, or almost anything else if you want to. I tend to reserve roasting for pork and chicken.

Roasting is pretty straightforward. Basically, you put a chicken, or a pork roast, or whatever else you're cooking into a roasting pan. You pre-heat the oven to the desired temperature, stick the roast in the oven for the prescribed time, take it out and check that it's done, then let it 'rest' for a few minutes and serve.

You will almost always chop some vegetables to go into the roasting pan as well. Putting them under and around the roast creates liquid in the pan which keeps the bottom from burning, and also allows the vegetables to cook in the juices from the roast, which can be very delicious.

Making a roast can be a little more on the challenging side in the beginning, if only because it can be difficult to find the balance between cooking the meat enough so that it's not raw in the middle, but not so much that it overcooks and gets dried out and flavorless. No two roasts are precisely the same size and shape, so there's always an element of guesswork in there, although you can eliminate much of that as you get used to it.

On the other hand, a roast usually leaves you with a lot of leftover meat that hasn't been tainted with additives, which can be very convenient to have around for lunch or dinner the next day.

Rotisserie

Although it's not found in every kitchen or grill, a rotisserie can be a great way to cook pork, chicken, or other roasts.

One of the problems with roasting is that it's difficult to make sure that the roast cooks evenly, and also some of the juices will run out of the roast while it's cooking. In a rotisserie, the roast is constantly rotating, which ensures that the roast cooks evenly, and also helps to keep the juices in the meat without dripping off.

You'll want to follow the instructions of your rotisserie oven or grill, but basically you tie up the chicken or roast with cooking twine if necessary, spear it, put it on the spit, and start it rotating. Then, cook more or less as normal over a drip pan with some liquid in it. After the prescribed amount of time, check for doneness and serve.

Again, if this is something you'd like to do, you'll need to check the directions on your specific appliance.

Dehydration

Dehydration is an unusual cooking practice, but it's pretty awesome once you get the hang of it.

Basically, a dehydrator can allow you to take fresh fruit and turn it into a healthy, delicious snack with no added ingredients and a much longer shelf life.

To dehydrate fruit, you need to cut it into thin slices— pieces that are probably not more than a few millimeters thick. It's important that the slices not be thick, because you need to be able get all the moisture out of there. If the fruit is too thick, there will still be water in the middle of the fruit, and that moisture will lead to spoilage.

Once the fruit is sliced, lay it out on the racks of your dehydrator. Most dehydrators have quite a bit of room inside, so if you want you can make a large quantity of dehydrated fruit at one time.

Then, just put the rack into the dehydrator and turn it on. You can check the instruction manual that came with the dehydrator for the proper settings and time. Dehydration will take longer the more fruit is in there, and could easily take 24 hours or more.

If you cut the fruit thin enough and did a good job dehydrating it, the fact that there is no moisture left means you've got some real fruit snacks that will have a pretty long shelf life—and because they were 'cooked' at such a low temperature, the vast majority of the nutrition is still completely intact. I've done this with apples, strawberries, bananas, kiwis, and pineapple, to name a few.

A dehydrator basically works by blowing hot air (not too hot—usually between 100 and 150 degrees) through a bunch of racks with fruit on them. The warm air constantly blowing past the fruit eventually pulls almost all of the moisture out of them.

If you make use of it, a dehydrator can be a great investment and a way to keep healthy and tasty fresh fruit snacks around all the time. Just read the instructions and give it a shot.

COMPONENTS OF A MEAL

In a couple of chapters you're going to learn a variety of recipes, but before that we need to talk about how to build a healthy meal. This is one of those situations where a lot of different purists and 'experts' will claim that there is one right way to go in this situation—your meal has to consist of exactly this amount of exactly these foods, or you're never going to be healthy.

It doesn't work that way. There have been billions of healthy people throughout human history, and they didn't all eat the exact same meals. However, it's still beneficial to talk in general about what goes in to a healthy meal.

Protein

Most protein that most people get is going to come from meat, and most meals in most homes are going to include some quantity of meat on any given day.

This can be fish, chicken, pork, beef, etc. A lot of people spend a lot of time worrying about fat and cholesterol in meat. If I were you, I would worry more about artificial flavorings and preservatives in some prepared meat products, which means only buying meat without such ingredients—more on that later.

Another option if you don't want to eat meat is eggs, which are high in protein and other nutrients. Of course, there is also dairy.

If you want a non-animal source of protein, look at beans (not soy) and lentils; these are a great, convenient source of protein and should be a regular part of any diet.

Carbohydrates

You probably know by now that carbohydrates are the fuel that keeps your body running. However, you may also think that the best source of carbohydrates for your body is going to be bread, pasta, or other starches.

Well, by far the best source of carbohydrates in your diet is going to be fresh fruit. If you want to be healthy, you need to make a point of eating a lot of fresh fruit every day.

You're probably not going to use fruit much when it comes to cooking, though, so vegetables will fulfill that need in your cooked meals (when I say vegetables, I am not talking about corn or potatoes, which you should think of as starches).

Although vegetables are not exactly loaded with carbs, they do provide a good amount, and the mainstream view of nutrition greatly exaggerates your need for carbs anyway. Although you absolutely need carbohydrates, you should get the majority in your diet from fresh fruit and not so much from starches. Almost anyone can improve their health by consuming fewer starches and more vegetables and fruits.

Oh—and beans and lentils are also a great, healthy source of carbohydrates, in addition to being a good source of protein.

Fat

This is the last of the three macronutrients, and certainly the most misunderstood. You need fat to be healthy, and you should not shy away from it. However, you do not need to create dishes centered around consuming fat—fat will be present in meat, eggs, and dairy, and you will use it to cook many of the dishes you make, so you should get all you need without having to go out of your way.

How To Build A Meal

Since we are talking about cooked meals here, for most people we're basically talking about dinner. Let's look at how to build a meal based on that.

Most dinners that you prepare will have 2-3 components on your plate. I recommend that one of those components be some variety of protein, and the remaining component or two be either beans or vegetables. Some example dinners might include roast pork with black beans and spinach, or a ribeye steak with butternut squash and green beans.

This meal structure means eating a lot of cooked vegetables, which a lot of people are usually not thrilled about. People tend to think of vegetables as not tasting like much, but that's usually because they think you aren't allowed to put anything else (like butter) on them to give them more flavor. I will show you how to cook vegetables in simple ways that make them delicious, so you'll actually look forward to eating them.

I used to focus a lot on meat when I ate, and—although I still enjoy it—once I actually learned how to cook vegetable and bean side dishes, I started to enjoy them as much as meat dishes, if not more.

So, that's what you'll use in your healthy dinners: a source of meat and/or beans, and 1-2 vegetables. Pretty simple, but it works.

MAKING COOKING CONVENIENT

We've spent some time already talking about skills that are specific to cooking, and of course we'll continue to do that in the rest of the book, both in general terms and with respect to specific recipes.

However, this book is not just about how to cook, it's also about how to incorporate cooking for yourself into everyday life.

I remember in my second year of college—which was my first year not living in the dorms—it took me a while to adjust to providing healthy food for myself. It feels weird to say it now, but there was a time when, every day around seven o'clock or so, I would just hop in the car and drive to a fast food place.

Basically, I wouldn't think about dinner until it was time to have it, and by that point it feels like you don't have time to do anything but go out and get something that somebody else already made—which, of course, tends to contain all kinds of unhealthy elements. That's basically the problem that gave rise to this whole book.

Later on, my then-girlfriend (now my wife) and I decided we needed to get healthier and start making food for ourselves. We still weren't used to keeping food on hand to make our own dinners, though, so almost every day we'd head to the supermarket at around six or seven to buy something to make for dinner.

As you can imagine, this made cooking dinner for ourselves a huge pain. Every day you have to drive to the supermarket, decide on something to make for yourself, bring it home and make it, eat it, and then clean everything up. It's not the sort of program most people would want to stick to, and this kind of inconvenience is exactly what sends people running to fast food places (or other more convenient, less healthy options) in the first place.

The bottom line is that while learning to cook for yourself is an important skill, it's not enough on its own. You also have to learn to incorporate cooking for yourself into your day-to-day life.

It's not hard to do, it just requires a little planning ahead. This will make your life much easier and your meals much healthier, and isn't that the whole point of this in the first place?

The resolution to this whole problem can be boiled down to two words: plan ahead.

That planning is going to have two major components. First, you need to plan your dinners out at least a few days in advance. That way, you'll already have the food you need on hand and you won't have to go to the store. Even if you decide to move the components of the meals around from one night to the next, you'll at least have what you need for all of those meals.

As a rule, when I go to the supermarket I like to make sure that I have what I need for at least the next three nights. That means I don't need to go food shopping more than about a couple of times a week. Of course, if you plan a little more you can go once a week or less.

Second, since keeping food on hand frequently means freezing some of it, you need to plan to thaw any frozen parts of the meal in the morning—typically meat or vegetables. Otherwise, dinner might roll around and your pork chops are frozen solid, which obviously poses a problem.

Basically, this means that when you get up in the morning, just take whatever you're planning to have for dinner out of the freezer and put it somewhere where it can thaw undisturbed. Larger items, like whole frozen chickens, probably need to be moved to the fridge the day before and then taken out the next day.

Another helpful habit to get into is portioning out food that you will freeze before it goes into the freezer. If you freeze a five-pound container of ground beef, but you only want one pound for your dinner, you'll have to thaw the whole thing and you'll end up with four extra pounds of beef.

To avoid this problem, just divide up the food you'll freeze (typically meat products) into one-dinner amounts. For example, for my wife and I, I freeze two pork chops, or two fish fillets, or two ribeyes together in plastic bags, since that is how many I'll use for dinner.

So it comes down to three pieces of advice:

1. Plan your meals out ahead of time, at least three days in advance for any trip to the store.

2. Divide frozen products into air-tight bags according to how much you need for one night.

3. Thaw any frozen parts of that night's dinner when you get up in the morning.

These three pieces of advice will make a world of difference if you're not used to cooking for yourself. They can be the difference between you making healthy meals for yourself and your family on a daily basis, and you and your family eating unnatural garbage every day. So, make a habit of following them, and you'll be able to make the most out of all the new skills and recipes you're learning from this book.

TRIAL AND ERROR

I've touched on this a couple of times so far, but I want to emphasize it a little more as we head into actually discussing recipes.

Many people who are learning how to cook are worried about doing it "wrong." If you're not used to cooking already, sometimes watching someone else cook makes it seem almost like magic, and you feel like if you were to try to do it, you wouldn't know just the right amount of everything to put in, and the meal would end up terrible.

But you don't need to know how to cook everything in the beginning. You only need to start by trying one thing. Then you'll get comfortable with that and move on to the next thing, and so on.

Start with a few simple flavors—like sea salt, black pepper, and butter or olive oil. These are flavors that almost everyone agrees taste good (and if you don't like one of them, you can just leave it out).

How To Cook

Begin by cooking anything—a vegetable, a meat, whatever—with these flavorings. Err on the side of not using enough, because it's better to underdo it than to overdo it, and you can always add a little more later. Once you're comfortable cooking with these flavors, add another flavor. An easy one to move to is garlic powder. Next time you cook up some onions or chicken or whatever, add in a little garlic powder. Again, remember to start by adding a little bit. After you taste the food, you may want to add more, just don't overdo it in the beginning.

So now you can cook with sea salt, black pepper, olive oil, butter, and garlic powder. Guess what—that's approximately half the flavoring battle right there. At this point, you may be happy. If you are, fine. You don't need to go any farther if you don't want to.

However, I would recommend continuing to branch out and experimenting with other flavors. Do you like Mexican food? Spend five minutes searching online about spices used in Mexican food. You might see chili powder mentioned a lot. So, buy some chili powder and add some to the next thing you cook. After you eat that, decide if you should have used more or less. Maybe you've noticed a lot of recipes use paprika. So get some paprika (I would recommend sweet Hungarian paprika, which you can find in most grocery stores) and try it out. If you like citrus flavors—I do—you might want to add lemon or lime juice to something. So do it!

If you feel uncomfortable cooking, just follow two simple rules. First, don't add more than one new flavor to any one dish that you make. That way, you can find out how you feel about the new flavor, and if you should use more or less next time. Second, err on the side of using too little of any new seasoning. Don't be afraid of it or anything, just don't pour it on there. If you eat the dish and find that you like the flavor, there just wasn't enough of it, then you can add more the next time.

Over time, you will come to be more and more comfortable using a variety of flavors, and you will get comfortable combining them and experimenting with new ones.

When it comes to baking (which we won't discuss in this book), it's important for most people to follow a recipe to make sure that whatever you're baking rises properly and cooks for the right amount of time and ends up how it's supposed to when it comes out of the oven. For most other kinds of cooking, though, the recipes are much more flexible and can easily be adjusted according to your own personal tastes. If a recipe calls for a certain amount of garlic, but you know that you like a little more or less, you can adjust accordingly without worrying that it's going to ruin the dish.

The best thing to do is get started by following someone else's simple recipe, which is what we'll be looking at in the next part of this book. Once you're comfortable cooking that, you can branch out and learn on your own how to cook a meal that you like. Maybe you'll stick with that simple recipe forever, maybe it will change completely over time. There's no wrong way to do it, and in the end it's all up to you.

Oh, and accept the idea that, especially in the beginning, every meal won't turn out exactly how you wanted it to. Don't worry about it. That's a part of the process, and you'll get better and better at it more quickly than you might think.

RECIPES

There are a lot of resources out there that you can use to find recipes, and the primary purpose of this book is not to provide recipes to you. Instead, the primary purpose is to teach what is good and bad in general when you cook, so that you can find and create good recipes yourself from now on, or tweak bad ones so they only contain natural, healthy ingredients.

After all, the ability to determine which other recipes are good or bad—and to make the bad ones good whenever possible—is much more valuable than a limited list of recipes.

However, there is still something to be said for having a list of recipes you can use to start out. In the beginning, it's nice to have a set of safe, easy recipes to get comfortable with. That's what these are—basic recipes you can begin with until you are comfortable cooking food for yourself. We'll cover a little bit of everything—main courses, side dishes, and other useful components that will allow you to make delicious, healthy meals.

The recipes are listed roughly in this order: main dishes/protein, side dishes, sauces, drinks.

BROILED STEAK

This is something I tend to do a couple of times a week with either ribeyes (my favorite) or sirloin.

Ingredients

Steak of your choice
Seasonings of your choice

1. Season the steak according to your preference. As always, a good basic approach is just a light coat of sea salt and pepper, maybe also with some soy sauce and/or garlic powder, but feel free to experiment.

2. Set your oven to high broil and allow a couple of minutes to warm up.

3. Place the steak on a broiling pan, and then put it into the oven at a level so that it's about 4 inches from the broiler in the top of your oven. Leave the oven door open a few inches.

4. Allow steak to cook around 3-7 minutes, depending on your preference, how hot your broiler gets, and how far the steak is from the heating element. Then, using heat-resistant tongs (or just a fork), flip the steaks and cook for a further 2-5 minutes on the other side.

****

If you don't have any experience cooking steaks, it might take you a couple of tries before you get the right level of 'doneness.' I like my steaks extremely rare, but of course eating raw or undercooked meats carries a risk of getting sick, so use your own judgment if you decide to cook your steak lightly.

BROILED FISH

This seems like a logical thing to jump into after discussing broiling steak, so let's do it.

Ingredients

Fish of your choice
Seasonings of your choice

1. Season fish to your liking—a good start might be sea salt, pepper, and olive oil (enough to coat the fish).

2. Turn your broiler on to high or low heat, depending on your preference (if you don't have a preference, just pick one and see how you like it).

3. After allowing the broiler to heat up for a couple of minutes, place the fish on the broiling pan, skin-side down (if there is skin), and put it in the oven so that fish fillets are about 4 inches from the heating element. Leave the oven door open a few inches.

4. Cook about 4-5 minutes on one side for fillets that aren't more than half an inch thick; fillets at this thickness typically only need to be cooked on one side. The fish should flake when it's done. For thicker fillets, broil skin-side up for 4-5 minutes, then turn the fish and cook for an additional 4 or 5 minutes on the other side. Timing will depend on the thickness of the fillet; try to avoid overcooking and drying out the fish.

****

How long it takes to cook will depend on the thickness and type of fish fillet, and the specifics of your oven. Be sure to cut into the thickest part of the fish after cooking to ensure that it's cooked all the way through.

This is a generic recipe that will work for just about any fish fillet, and as always, feel free to improvise with other flavors. Some really good flavors to add to this or any fish recipe include butter, lemon, paprika, and balsamic vinegar, so feel free to add any of those to the seasonings you use to coat the fish before you cook it. If you're not used to cooking fish, it will take a few tries to get the timing down so you find a balance between cooking the fish all the way and not drying it out by cooking too much.

As a side note, I think seasoned, broiled salmon skin is one of the most delicious things there is.

ROASTED CHICKEN

I don't eat a lot of chicken myself, but roasting a chicken can be a great way to cook a meat dish and some flavorful vegetables in the same pan, and the roasted chicken skin is extremely delicious. Also, you'll probably have some chicken left over you can use for lunch the next day.

If your chicken is frozen, make sure it's fully defrosted in time for dinner! You can move it from the freezer to the fridge the night before and then take it out in the morning to defrost; that should do it.

Ingredients

4.5 pound chicken
1-3 onions, sliced
Carrots and/or celery, skinned and chopped (optional)
Fat/oil of your choice
Seasonings of your choice

1. Preheat your oven to 450 degrees.

2. Chop up a few onions, and also some carrots and/or celery if you like (if you're going to add celery, be sure to peel it because the celery skin can get surprisingly tough during roasting). Lay the vegetables in the bottom of a roasting pan.

3. Over the sink, remove your chicken from its wrapping, remove the giblets from the inside, and rinse and pat the inside and outside dry with paper towels.

4. Coat the chicken with butter or olive oil, then rub with sea salt and pepper.

5. Feel free to insert whole herbs or half lemons inside the chicken if you like, but you don't have to. Lay the chicken on top of the vegetables in the roasting pan.

6. Put the chicken in the oven, and immediately turn the oven down to 400 degrees. Cook a 4.5 pound chicken for about 90 minutes, or until the juice runs clear, and/or a thermometer in the thigh (but not touching the bone) registers 160 degrees.

****

Remove the roasting pan from the oven and let it rest 5-15 minutes. Serve the chicken and the vegetables together, and don't be shy about spooning out some of the chicken drippings over your plate. Also, save the drippings for later, because they're great to cook with. Add some drippings to just about anything that you're cooking in a frying pan for a big shot of savory flavor.

ROAST PORK

Like a roasted chicken, roast pork is a good way to prepare a large quantity of food at one time—including vegetables in the roasting pan—and it typically gives you a lot of additive-free leftover meat you can use in lunches or other meals for a couple of days.

Ingredients

2-pound pork tenderloin
Onions, chopped
Carrots and/or celery, skinned and chopped (optional)
Fat/Oil of your choice
Seasonings of your choice

1. Preheat your oven to 350 degrees.

2. As with the chicken, chop up a few onions, and some carrots and/or celery if you like (as before, if you're going to add celery, be sure to peel it). Lay the vegetables in the bottom of a roasting pan.

3. Over the sink, remove your pork from its wrapping. Place it on a plate or in a shallow bowl.

4. Coat the pork with melted butter and/or olive oil, then rub with salt and pepper and any other seasoning you like (some recommendations include garlic powder, chili powder, turmeric, or paprika, or even honey and/or mustard).

5. Lay the tenderloin on top of the vegetables in the roasting pan.

6. Put the pan in the oven and cook for about 80-90 minutes, or until a meat thermometer in the middle of the roast registers 145 degrees. For best results, turn the pork a few times during cooking, and spoon some juices over the top of it to keep it from drying out.

7. Remove the pork and let it rest, covered, for 15 minutes. When you slice into the thickest part of the pork, it should be white, or ideally JUST BARELY pink inside—that way you know it's cooked, but it should still be juicy and flavorful.

****

It takes a few tries to 'get to know' your oven a little bit until you know how long to cook a roast so that it's all the way done but not overcooked. Just cut into the thickest part of the pork and check to see that the inside is white or just slightly pink in the very center, and if it isn't, put it back in for another five or ten minutes as appropriate. Of course, a larger roast will need to cook longer.

PAN-FRIED FISH

Pan-fried fish is a great option for a quick, light protein source for your meal.

Ingredients

Fish of your choice
Oil of your choice
Seasonings of your choice

1. Place raw fish on a plate or in a bowl. Pour over enough olive oil or peanut oil to just coat the fish. Season to your liking, and rub the seasoning to cover the fish evenly. The coating of oil will help keep the seasoning on the fish.

2. Heat 2-3 tbsp of fat/oil in a pan over medium-low to medium heat.

3. Cook fish through in the pan, around 3 minutes a side for thinner fillets and 4 or 5 minutes a side for thicker fillets.

****

That's about it! When the fish is done you can add a little bit of wine and/or lemon juice to what's left in the pan and cook it for another few minutes to make a simple sauce. If you use wine, be sure to cook off the alcohol; more on that later.

PAN-FRIED PORK CHOP

Pan-fried pork chops can be extremely delicious—the key is to cook them enough so they're cooked through, but not so much that they get dry and tough.

Ingredients

Pork chops of your choice (I like rib chops)
Oil of your choice
Seasonings of your choice

1. Place raw pork chops on a plate or in a bowl. Pour over enough olive oil or peanut oil to just coat the pork. Season to your liking, and rub the seasoning to cover the pork evenly. The coating of oil will help keep the seasoning on the pork.

2. Heat 2-3 tbsp of fat/oil in a pan over medium heat. Be sure to let oil heat thoroughly—the oil should move in the pan like water when you tilt the pan to one side or the other.

3. Cook the pork 4-5 minutes on each side. When you cut into the chop, it should be no more than <u>just barely</u> pink inside. That means it's cooked enough to be safe, but it's still juicy and tasty. This will take a few tries to get right, and if the chop is any more than just barely pink, you need to throw it back onto the frying pan.

****

Whether you're making a pork roast or pan-frying pork chops, cooking them for just the right amount of time is key for ideal flavor. Raw pork is not safe to eat, and pork that's overcooked can get dry and tough pretty quickly. It'll take you a few tries to find the balance, but it's well worth it.

SIMPLE CHILI

Chili is awesome. This is a simple chili recipe which you can tweak as much as you like to suit your tastes.

Ingredients

2 tbsp butter
1 large onion, chopped
1 bell pepper, chopped (optional)
1 pound ground or chopped beef
1 can black beans (approximately 15 ounces)
1 can diced tomatoes (approximately 15 ounces)
1 tbsp chili powder
1 tbsp cumin
1/2 tsp cayenne pepper (optional)
Sea salt and pepper to taste

1. Melt butter on medium heat in a medium-to-large pot.

2. Throw in chopped onions and peppers (if you're using them). Cook until the onions are translucent.

3. Add chili powder, cumin, cayenne (if you want a little spice), and salt and pepper. Stir thoroughly and cook a further two minutes or so.

4. Throw in ground or chopped beef—sometimes I like to make this with sirloin that I chop to approximately half-inch to three-quarter inch cubes.

5. Stir in and cook beef, making sure to coat it with the seasonings in the pot, around four more minutes. Also, make sure to break up the meat before it all cooks if you're using ground beef, so you don't end up with big chunks of meat in your chili.

6. Drain the black beans and add them to the pot. Add the tomatoes as well—you can completely or only partially drain the tomato juice, according to your preference. Stir in, then turn the burner to low and let sit covered for around 20 minutes.

****

There is a lot of flexibility in this recipe. Personally, I add more seasoning than this, but you should start with something along these lines and then add what you like—garlic powder, more cumin and/or chili powder and/or cayenne pepper, whatever. Don't like black beans? Make it with kidney beans. Just check the can and make sure you're not adding in any undesirable additives. If you want more or less beef, adjust accordingly.

You may find that there's more liquid than you'd like in the chili. If so, uncover it and turn the heat up a little until water starts to steam out of the chili and the level of liquid is more to your liking.

If you want to make it with chicken or pork you can do that too—just throw in leftover chicken or pork, or add it raw and be sure to cook it all the way through.

Start with this basic version, but feel free to make it your own. That's true of every recipe in here, but particularly true for the chili.

FRIED EGG

This is one of the simplest, most basic things to cook, and it's plenty tasty as well. One cool thing about a fried egg is that it's one of few common dishes that give people an opportunity to consume raw animal protein, as long as you leave the yolk runny. Of course, remember that there is always some risk associated with eating raw animal products, and if you don't like it or feel comfortable with it, there's no reason to force yourself to eat it that way.

Ingredients

1 egg
2 tbsp butter

1. Melt butter in a frying pan pan over low-medium to medium heat.

2. Once the butter is thoroughly heated, crack the egg over the pan.

3. Cook until the translucent, liquid egg white becomes solid and opaque, and until the yolk achieves desired rawness or firmness.

****

This is the sort of thing that takes about a minute to learn how to do correctly, and a lifetime to learn how to do just right. If you like the yolk firm, then it's pretty easy—just let the egg cook until the whole thing is firm. If you like the yolk less cooked, then it's all about the balance between cooking the white and trying not to cook the yolk.

If you want the yolk as raw as possible—like I do—the absolute most reliable way to do this is to separate the yolk from the white, cook the white first, and then just lay the yolk on top when the white is basically done, just long enough so the yolk warms slightly. It's a little more of a pain, but it's the only guarantee of a perfectly cooked white and a perfectly runny yolk.

If you're looking for something in between, just experiment to find the technique and timing that most consistently produces the kind of yolk you like.

SAUTÉED VEGETABLES

These are pretty much a staple in any healthy dinner, and they're very straightforward to prepare. This simple, basic dish can be made with fresh vegetables (always the best choice) as well as frozen or canned vegetables (both still good choices, as long as they're additive-free).

Ingredients

Fresh, frozen, or canned vegetable of your choice
2 tbsp fat/oil of your choice
Seasonings of your choice

1. Chop, open, or defrost vegetables, whichever is necessary. Drain extra liquid, if applicable.

2. Heat about two tablespoons of the fat/oil of your choice in a frying pan over low-medium to medium heat. Feel free to add a little more for flavor if necessary.

3. Throw in your vegetables.

4. Add seasoning of your choice (as described in "Trial And Error"). A good basic start would be some sea salt and black pepper, and maybe a little garlic powder.

5. Cook through for around 5-15 minutes, depending on the vegetable and your personal preferences.

****

I know this is a very generalized recipe, but it will cover a whole variety of situations, and in the end it's all going to come down to the vegetables you enjoy preparing anyway. A very important aspect of sticking to a healthy diet is variety, and you can use this basic recipe with almost any vegetable in the grocery store.

You can just walk through the produce section, or past the frozen or canned vegetables, and pick pretty much anything you see. I like to use this with fresh onions, bell peppers, or mushrooms; with canned peas, green beans, or spinach; and with frozen spinach, butternut squash, and broccoli, to name just a few. Try a few things, experiment with flavors and cooking time and heat, and find out what you like.

STEAMED VEGETABLES

Steamed vegetables are convenient and healthy, and can even taste pretty good with just a little bit of salt, pepper, and butter on them. You can make them with a vegetable steamer or a steamer basket, although in my opinion a vegetable steamer is a lot easier and more convenient.

Ingredients

Chopped fresh vegetables
Water
Sea salt and black pepper to taste
Butter to taste

1. Put your steamer basket in the bottom of a pot. Fill the pot with water almost to the bottom of the steamer basket.

2. Bring the water to a boil and then add your vegetables. Cover with a lid tilted so that a little steam can escape.

3. Steam vegetables and remove when done. Most vegetables steam in 4-6 minutes, although thicker and denser vegetables may need to steam longer. Of course, adjust the time to your personal tastes if you like the vegetables a little firmer or a little softer.

4. Once the vegetables come out, melt some butter over them and flavor them with sea salt and pepper according to your tastes.

****

Those are the instructions for a steamer basket. If you'd like to use a rice cooker/vegetable steamer like the one I recommended earlier in the book, follow the instructions that accompany your appliance. Typically, this will mean putting a prescribed amount of water in the steamer, putting the vegetables in their basket, closing the lid and pressing a button.

I always use my vegetable steamer, but of course either one works just as well.

BASIC BEANS

There are a million different ways to make beans (or lentils), and you can even use the "Sautéed Vegetables" recipe on canned beans if you like.

However, this is one simple way that I like to prepare canned beans—particularly black beans, since I love the taste and they tend to have no undesirable additives.

Ingredients

1 small onion, chopped
1 15 ounce can of black beans, drained
1/2 stick of butter
Sea salt and black pepper to taste
Garlic powder to taste

1. Melt butter in a sauce pan over medium heat.

2. Throw in the onion and cook until soft and translucent.

3. Season with salt, pepper, and garlic powder. Mix in the seasoning.

4. Add the beans, turn to medium-low heat and let sit covered for 15 minutes or so, checking and stirring periodically.

5. When the beans are hot all the way through, mash them up a little bit in the pan. I like to mash them enough so that they're a little bit like mashed potatoes. Don't spend all day doing it, just a few minutes so that the liquid from the onion, and the butter, and the spices all get incorporated in to the mashed beans.

****

That's it—you've now got a surprisingly tasty side dish you can make with just about any kind of bean (or with peas as well, for that matter). You can add some stock (though you probably want to reduce the liquid), or you can add chili powder or garlic, or all three. There's a lot of flexibility with this dish, and it's got a lot of good, natural nutrition too.

SIMPLE VEGETABLE SOUP

Vegetable soup is a delicious, versatile, and surprisingly easy thing to make—and, of course, it's a great option on a cold day.

Ingredients

3 cups chopped vegetables of your choice
3 tbsp fat/oil of your choice
Soy sauce to taste
Sea salt and pepper to taste
1 cup stock

1. Heat your fat over medium heat. I would recommend using olive oil, butter, or a combination of the two.

2. Add the vegetables, then add soy sauce, sea salt, and pepper to taste.

3. When the vegetables are cooked to your liking, add stock and bring to a boil. Then, cover, turn down to low,

and let simmer for 15-20 minutes. This recipe makes about 3 servings.

****

As is the case with the other recipes in this book, this is an extremely simple version of vegetable soup. For more flavorful soup, add some dry white wine (1/2 cup or so) after step 2 and cook until the wine is reduced.

There is a lot of flexibility here, and as always you should learn to cook this dish to your tastes by varying seasonings and cooking time.

You can use just onions here if you want, or any combination of onions, broccoli, carrots, peas, mushrooms, cabbage, etc. Canned beans are a great option for a more filling soup with some protein, and a can of diced tomatoes adds a great flavor and color to your broth. Try whatever sounds good to you—just bear in mind that firmer vegetables, like carrots, will take more time to cook through and soften up, so you should try cut them in relatively thin pieces and give them time to cook all the way so that you don't end up with crunchy carrots in your soup.

BASIC SALAD

A salad is a pretty simple concept, but unfortunately almost every salad dressing is made with unhealthy oils. This is a way to throw together an easy, tasty, healthy salad without depending on one of those store-bought dressings.

Ingredients

Chopped romaine lettuce
1-2 tbsp olive oil
Sea salt and black pepper to taste
Balsamic vinegar to taste (optional)
Parmesan cheese to taste (optional)
Anchovies (optional)

1. Toss everything together in a bowl.

2. Eat it.

****

See? I told you it was easy. This is approximately right for one person, so add more olive oil if you're making more than one serving.

I know it's simple, but it can be very flavorful. Don't be afraid to add some more olive oil and Parmesan cheese if it suits your tastes.

If you've never really tried anchovies, you should give them a shot. They're very savory and delicious, and if you chop them up into a salad you don't even really notice the texture, just the savory flavor. If you do try anchovies, get the kind that are just packed in olive oil and salt. Read the ingredients to make sure you aren't introducing any additives into your salad.

QUINOA

I'm not big on grains, but most people are used to eating something along these lines with their dinner, and quinoa has a lot to recommend it compared to other grains—it's gluten-free and has more protein than any other grain, and can be prepared in a way that's very similar to rice.

Ingredients

1 cup quinoa
2 cups water

1. Combine quinoa and water in a sauce pan.

2. Bring to a vigorous boil, then turn to low heat, cover, and simmer for around fifteen minutes, or until the quinoa is tender, chewy, and little white spirals form around each grain.

****

How To Cook

You can serve quinoa with butter, sea salt, and pepper, and it's pretty delicious. Although it's healthier than most other grains, you still shouldn't go overboard and load up on it, especially if you're trying to watch your weight.

Also, by far the easiest way to make quinoa is just to put it into a rice cooker, in a 2:1 water-to-quinoa ratio, and press "cook." Every rice cooker is different, but this works great in mine and it's very easy.

YOGURT DRESSING

This is a very simple, very versatile yogurt sauce/dressing. I like it on just about anything savory, hot or cold.

Ingredients

16 oz. plain whole fat yogurt
1-3 raw garlic cloves, finely chopped
1-2 tbsp lemon juice
Fresh dill, chopped (optional)
Sea salt and/or pepper to taste (optional)

1. Combine all ingredients.

****

As always, adjust this to your own tastes; you can use as much or as little garlic as you like. I prefer this dressing with fresh dill, but it still tastes good without it.

SIMPLE GRAVY

Is there anybody who doesn't love good gravy? Probably not.

Ingredients

Pan drippings
1 cup dry white wine
1 cup stock
Sea salt and pepper to taste
Other seasonings to taste

1. After you've cooked any meat, you should have some drippings left over in the pan. If they're already in a frying pan, great. If they're in a roasting pan, then pour off as much fat as you can (the fat will be the clear stuff on top) into a separate container, and then pour the darker, more opaque drippings into a frying pan or sauce pan.

2. With your pan on medium heat, pour in the wine. Be sure to scrape up any brown bits that may be stuck to the

pan from whatever you were cooking it. These little bits pack a ton of flavor.

3. After you've scraped up all the little bits, add the stock. Add any seasonings you like, then turn the heat up to medium-high or high heat and reduce at least until the volume goes down by half. As always, do not reduce so long that you cook out all the moisture, or you could ruin your gravy and your pan.

****

That's it—you're now able to make gravy without resorting to any scary, mysterious brown substance in a bottle. This gravy will not be quite as thick as some gravies, but it will be very flavorful and delicious, and it also will not slowly kill you with weird additives. So, that's a plus.

GUACAMOLE

I love guacamole. It's one of the easiest dips you can make, and it uses only natural, whole ingredients. There's some flexibility on the quantities here, but try to keep approximately these ratios.

Ingredients

3 ripe avocados
2 Roma tomatoes, chopped
1/2 small onion, finely chopped
Sea salt to taste
Juice of 1 lime

1. Remove skin and pit from avocados and mash them up in a medium-to-large bowl.

2. Mix in chopped tomatoes and onions.

3. Mix in salt and lime juice to taste.

****

If you've only got two avocados, or you want to use three tomatoes, this recipe will still work. My only word of warning would be not to overdo it too much with the onion, because the raw onion can start to overpower the other flavors. Other than that, just go with your gut.

Fresh guacamole doesn't keep well, because avocado that's exposed to air for a little while starts to oxidize and turn a brownish/grayish color. If you want to save some in the fridge for the next day, just press some plastic wrap flush up to the surface of the guacamole so that none of it is exposed to the air, and it will keep reasonably well.

If some part does turn brown due to exposure to air, you can just skim it off with a spoon, and what's underneath should still be fine.

The whole key to guacamole is finding perfectly ripe avocados, which can be a challenge. A ripe avocado should be a dark brownish/purplish color on the outside, and should be pretty soft to the touch, but not completely mushy.

Some grocery stores will carry ripe avocados, but in my experience even ones that look ripe in the store are never quite right. I prefer to buy the avocados when they are hard and green, and then store them at room temperature in a small paper bag with the top rolled closed for around 3-5 days to ripen. If you stick a banana in there too, they will ripen faster.

Once ripe, you can use them immediately or store them in the fridge for a few days. The flesh of a ripe avocado should be yellow toward the middle and green toward the skin, and it should be soft enough to mash up, but not soft enough that it starts to be brown and mushy.

You'll get the hang of it after you try a few avocados, but just bear in mind that the ripeness of the avocados is the absolute key to making good guacamole, and going the extra mile to get the good ones is totally worth it.

LEMONADE

Water is, by far, the healthiest thing you can drink. But, it can get a little boring sometimes, and the last thing you want to do is lapse into drinking soda or (God forbid) diet soda, or who knows what else.

So, when water gets boring, you can turn to these next few recipes for healthy, natural, tasty drinks. We'll start with lemonade.

Ingredients

6 ounces raw honey or 3 ounces raw agave nectar
4 ounces of lemon juice, or the juice of about 3 lemons
    (seeds removed)
1 cup water

1. Throw it all in the blender, and blend until thoroughly mixed.

2. Pour the mixture into a pitcher (approximately 64 ounces) and fill the rest of the way with water, making sure it's thoroughly mixed.

3. Stick it in the fridge, or serve it with ice.

****

Well, that was easy. As always, if you want it to be sweeter or tarter, add more honey or lemon juice, respectively. Also, honey can be a pain to measure since it's so thick and sticky, so you might want to learn to eyeball the amount and put it straight into the blender to make it easier.

Don't start out with cold water, because the honey is much harder to mix in cold water. Make sure the water is room-temperature.

Fresh lemons are always best, but this is a great opportunity to use that frozen, pure lemon juice we talked about earlier if you don't have fresh lemons. It's easy to keep on hand and doesn't contain any unnatural stuff.

Feel free to add or substitute limes in this recipe for a slight twist on the flavor.

ORANGE JUICE

A typical juicer is cool, but a little bit of a pain—you lose a lot of the fruit in the juicing process, you have to clean it afterward which tends to be a chore—there's a lot to be said for juicing your own fruit, but not a lot of people do it on a regular basis.

This is where a citrus juicer comes in. A great advantage of having a citrus juicer over a typical juicer is that they're a lot cheaper, they're a lot easier to clean, and they get more juice out of each piece of fruit. So don't overlook fresh orange juice! With a decent citrus juicer it's pretty easy to make and clean up, and the juice is extremely healthy as well as delicious.

Ingredients

Oranges

1. Slice oranges in half through the middle.

2. Thoroughly juice each orange half.

****

See? Easy. Of course, you can make grapefruit juice as well. The flavor is a bit of an acquired taste, but grapefruit is very good for you, and you can mix in raw honey (or mix orange and grapefruit juice) if you're not a fan of the bitterness.

Do you like orange soda? Get a bottle of club soda or other carbonated water without additives, and try a glass of half carbonated water and half fresh orange juice.

SWEET GREEN TEA

There are a lot of people who owe poor health in part to consuming a lot of sweet tea. This is because normal sweet tea is loaded with huge amounts of (at best) processed white sugar and (at worst) some combination of corn syrup and other sweeteners and additives.

If you want to drink something flavorful besides water, you can make a better version of sweet tea.

Ingredients

3-4 green tea bags
Raw honey or agave nectar to taste
Hot water
Lemon juice (optional)

1. Put four green tea bags in a mug.

2. Heat water in a kettle.

3. When the water in the kettle is ready, pour it into the mug.

4. Let the tea sit for at least 3 or 4 minutes, swirling the tea bags around a few times so the water circulates, then remove the tea bags.

5. Allow the tea in the mug to cool until near room temperature—you don't want to pour raw honey into very hot tea, or the high temperature will damage some of nutrients in the raw honey.

6. When the tea is sufficiently cooled, mix in the desired amount of raw honey—probably 1/4 cup to 1/2 cup, or about half that amount if you're using agave nectar instead.

7. Transfer the concentrated tea and honey mixture from the mug into a pitcher (approximately 64 ounces). Fill the rest of the way with water, and make sure you mix everything up thoroughly, then stick it in the refrigerator.

****

Of course, if you want stronger tea, use more tea bags or less water, and you can vary the amount of honey according to your tastes. You can also add in some lemon juice at the end if you like.

If you don't like the flavor of honey and just want something sweet, you can try using raw agave nectar, though it's about twice as sweet as honey, so you'll typically use half as much.

I'll say this one more time—there are people out there who suck down sweet tea all day long, and that's not a good idea no matter what the recipe is. This is supposed to be a change of pace if you don't like drinking water all the time. Just because it's a better recipe doesn't mean you should have it all day every day, but making it every so often is no problem at all.

BREAKFAST SMOOTHIE

This is a great way to have a healthy breakfast that doesn't take long. Most mornings I have something like this for breakfast.

Ingredients

1 banana
Approx. 1/2 cup whole fat plain yogurt
Approx. 2 tbsp raw honey or 1 tbsp raw agave nectar
Approx. 1/2 cup frozen fruit (blueberries, strawberries, etc.)
1-2 tbsp cocoa powder (optional)

1. Combine ingredients in blender.

2. Blend until smooth.

****

As always, this recipe is very flexible, so feel free to experiment. Just make sure the fruit you use is additive-free.

If smoothies become a regular part of your life, you might consider getting a Blendtec blender—this is what I use, and though it's pretty expensive, nothing else does the job quite like it.

CHOCOLATE MILK

It doesn't matter how old you are, everybody loves chocolate milk. Here's a recipe with only natural ingredients you can make in your blender in less than a minute.

Ingredients

8 ounces of organic whole milk
2 tbsp cocoa powder
2 tbsp raw honey OR 1 tbsp raw agave nectar
1 banana (optional)

1. Put everything in the blender, and blend thoroughly.

****

This makes approximately one serving, so, of course, multiply these numbers times the number of servings you'd like.

Adding the banana is optional, but I like the flavor and I like adding a piece of raw fruit into the mix. You can also blend in a few blueberries or strawberries if you like.

If you're the sort of person who likes dark chocolate (I am), you might want to go a little heavier with the cocoa. When I make this I don't actually measure it out, so feel free to eyeball it when you have a better sense of the way you like it.

LEAFY FRUIT SMOOTHIE

There's a lot of talk lately about "green" smoothies—smoothies that involve green leafy vegetables. They are certainly quite healthy in general, but they tend to be something less than delicious, which means most people won't stick to them.

Also, a lot of greens are tough to blend, so unless you've got a really good blender, you'll probably end up with a mixture that doesn't taste so great and also needs to be chewed on the way down.

This is a simple way to enjoy the benefits of a green smoothie—that's surprisingly tasty—without needing a super-duper blender.

Ingredients

Chopped watermelon
Fresh spinach

1. Put watermelon in the blender first, then spinach on top in a watermelon-to-spinach ratio of about 2:1.

2. Blend thoroughly.

****

You may need to stop blending intermittently and press the ingredients down into the blender in the beginning, and depending on your blender you may even need to add a little water to get things moving, but once the watermelon gets going, there should be plenty of liquid in there and it should blend fine.

This is a great, refreshing drink and an awesome way to get a big dose of fresh fruit and vegetables. With a decent blender, you can throw in a few grapes or strawberries too, although most typical blenders might have trouble blending them until smooth.

****

That's it! You've now got a full set of straightforward, versatile recipes you should feel confident trying no matter what your experience level. And in case I didn't say it enough already, make them your own! The first time through you should more or less stick to the recipe as described, but after that, don't be afraid to try some different things!

If you really want to be able to cook decent food for yourself on an ongoing basis, you'll need to learn more about which flavors and flavor combinations you like most. There's not really any way to do that besides just trying different things and seeing how they go.

One thing to look out for—try not to over-salt things. It's easy to add too much salt—especially if you're relatively new to cooking—and nothing ruins a dish faster or more reliably than adding too much of it. It's very easy to add salt at the table, and very hard to take it out once it's in there. When in doubt, use a little less, at least until you've got a little more experience under your belt.

Now that you've got a basic arsenal to work with, let's move on to the next topic...

HOW TO FIND A HEALTHY RECIPE ONLINE

I could go on and on with more recipes, but we'll stop here for two reasons:

1) This covers the basics, and you should be able to tweak these recipes in a lot of different ways to achieve the flavors you like and to create a whole variety of different dishes.

2) The internet is already overflowing with recipes, from simple recipes on free websites to more sophisticated ones in cookbooks and other resources.

3) I don't know you! You might not even like this stuff, and you need to know the best way to find other recipes on your own.

What I think is more valuable in this situation than a longer list of recipes is, instead, some tips on what to look for (and what to avoid) when you do search for recipes elsewhere, and advice on how to change other recipes, when possible, to make them more healthy and natural.

Let's say you're looking for a recipe that falls outside of what we've talked about in this book. If you're like most people, you'll go online and start searching for whatever it is you have in mind—"spicy pork chops" or "mushroom casserole" or whatever. You're probably going to find a bunch of different recipes from a bunch of different websites. Unfortunately, most of those recipes will probably go against what we've learned in this book, and they will contain ingredients you want to avoid.

After all, a big benefit of making your own food is that you know about, and get to control, everything that goes into a dish. Why ruin it by putting in the same crap you might get eating some kind of prepared food? It's potentially a big problem, but it's not so hard to fix. Just know what to look for, spend an extra five minutes finding it, and you'll be good to go.

Without further ado, let's take a look at the most common things you want to avoid, and how you can avoid them.

1) Unnatural Fats

This is a big one. As soon as a recipe says "take a tablespoon of vegetable oil..." you know you're in trouble. You can substitute in olive, peanut, or coconut oil, depending on which flavor you prefer. Peanut oil is a good choice in recipes because it has a high smoke point and its taste complements a range of other flavors, both sweet and savory.

2) Seasoning Mixes

Another red flag is a sentence that starts with "Open a packet of..." and tells you to dump some particular name brand of seasoning mix. These mixes are often loaded with MSG in different forms, preservatives, artificial colorings, and who knows what else. Always read the ingredients on any seasoning mix, and if you see anything besides the name of an actual spice, I would avoid it.

Big things to avoid are different versions of MSG, which can include disodium inosinate, 'autolyzed' or 'hydrolyzed' anything, any kind of protein concentrate or protein isolate, any kind of modified starch, any kind of yeast extract or protein extract. Any of these is a deal-breaker.

If you see this sort of thing in a recipe, you can do two things—find another recipe, or try to approximate what's in the spice packet based on what you've got in your kitchen. Either one can be fine; it's up to you.

If you want to approximate, just take a look at the ingredients and work from there. If one of the first ingredients is garlic powder, and there's also some chili powder and turmeric, well... use mostly garlic powder, with a little chili powder and turmeric. Also, try to make the amount of spices approximate the size of the packet, more or less—if the packet contains a tablespoon of total ingredients, add a similar amount of your own blend of spices.

It's pretty self-explanatory, but a lot of people who are not comfortable in the kitchen will be reluctant because they think they might ruin something. Just use common sense and give it a shot!

3) Pre-Seasoned Foods

This is another potential pitfall. A recipe might call for a can of some vegetable that is already seasoned, or might tell you to use some kind of sausage that is heavily seasoned, or you might pick up something from the butcher shop that's pre-seasoned.

You'll handle this in basically the same way as you handled the seasoning mix. Take a look at the ingredients —if all you see are the names of spices, you're good to go. If you see artificial crap in there (especially hidden MSG as discussed under Seasoning Mixes), don't use it.

In some situations, like if you see something at the butcher shop that's already seasoned and has no ingredient list, I would avoid it altogether, since you have no idea what's in there.

Again, you try to approximate the seasoning on your own using only ordinary spices. This usually does the job just fine, especially after you've tried this sort of thing once or twice and you get more comfortable with it.

4) Canned Soups, Stocks, and Broths

Many recipes call for stock or broth, or the use of some kind of canned soup (often "cream of" mushroom or broccoli or who knows what). We'll talk about canned soups first.

Most recipes that call for canned soups are basically shortcut recipes; instead of making some kind of simple sauce, you just throw in a can of soup that approximates the flavor and texture and go from there.

Well, canned soups are so packed with artificial flavors and different versions of MSG (even the ones that claim to contain no MSG) that I would avoid them entirely, especially ones with "cream of" something in the title. Just look for another recipe that does not use canned soup.

The next thing we need to discuss is stock, which is common in a lot of recipes. The best thing to do by far is to make your own stock, as described in this book (we'll get to that in a little while). However, even though most store-bought stock is something you want to stay far away from due to various types of MSG, a limited few are acceptable.

As with the seasoning packets, you need to read the label to avoid any bad stuff, and the primary offender will be different forms of MSG, which I'll describe here one more time so you can start to get familiar with them: they include disodium inosinate, 'autolyzed' or 'hydrolyzed' anything, any kind of protein concentrate or protein isolate, any kind of modified starch, and any kind of yeast extract or protein extract.

Don't eat them!

Checking out the labels might seem like a pain, but it just takes a few minutes, and once you find a product that fits the bill, you don't need to check the label anymore for that particular ingredient when you need to buy it in the future. The brand I use when I'm out of homemade stock is "Kitchen Basics," which seems to be in most major grocery stores.

5) Cooking Wine

A lot of recipes call for wine. A good rule of thumb, both for flavor and and health reasons, is not to cook with wine you wouldn't drink. In other words, don't buy a bottle of anything called "cooking wine," because it's basically just low quality wine that's loaded with salt. Just buy normal wine that you would drink, and cook with that according to the recipe.

****

Well, that covers the bases of most of the pitfalls you run into when you try to find recipes online or from other sources that might not exactly be natural and healthy. Now you know what to look out for when you cook so that all your meals can be healthy and free of artificial ingredients, which is great news for your long-term health.

HOW TO MAKE STOCK

Stock is an important ingredient for a number of reasons. It can add a great flavor to almost anything savory, and—while the MSG-laden stock you typically get from a store is not remotely healthy, and is something you should avoid completely—natural, "real" stock is loaded with minerals and other nutrients and is very healthy for you.

As previously mentioned, you can find brands of stock in the store that are okay, but it's always best to make your own. We'll talk about making chicken stock, because it's relatively straightforward and you can use it in almost anything.

In its simplest form, chicken stock is just chicken bones cooked for a long time in hot water. That's basically it—after a while, the hot water pulls a lot of the juices and nutrients out of the bones, and when you remove the bones, what you're left with is chicken stock. Ta da!

But, we're going to make it a little more interesting than that by adding some vegetables and seasonings. There are many different ways to make stock, and you shouldn't feel too limited by what's put forth here as long as you don't add anything unnatural to it.

Here's a basic set of ingredients:

1 roasted chicken carcass (whatever bones, etc. are left after you roast a chicken and you have removed all the meat that you want to eat)
About 2 tbsp apple cider vinegar
1 or 2 roughly chopped onions
3 or 4 roughly chopped celery stalks
3 or 4 skinned and roughly chopped carrots
5-20 peppercorns
1-3 bay leaves
Sea salt to taste

Again, all of these ingredients, except the chicken, are optional. You don't have any carrots? Leave them out. Not a fan of pepper? Use fewer peppercorns, or leave them out altogether. No big deal. It's up to you.

Put everything into a large stock pot. Put enough water in the pot to cover all the ingredients. Bring to a boil, then cover it and reduce it to a simmer, and let it sit, for a while —at least 8 hours. I actually cover mine and put it on low for at least a couple of days.

If a lot of water is cooking off, then you will need to add water to keep all the ingredients covered, and if you're going to leave it overnight, make sure the heat is low enough that the stock is not bubbling, or even really moving at all, just staying hot. If it's too hot and it boils away until it's dry, it will ruin your pot and possibly your stove, and leaving something alone that is that hot is dangerous anyway.

Of course, you need to make sure the stock pot is not accessible to any pets or children who might try to get to it, especially if you're leaving it for a long period or overnight.

After you're done cooking the stock, you'll need to strain out all the solid components. Either pour it through a strainer or colander into another large pot, or scoop out the solid parts with a strainer. Any way you do this is going to be a little bit of pain; just bite the bullet and do it. You'll get better at it.

Once you've removed all the solids, congratulations, you've made you're first batch of stock! There's probably a lot of it, which can make it difficult to store; that's why you're going to reduce it.

That means you put the pot back on the stove and turn the heat back up high enough to start a low boil. As the water cooks off, you'll be left with a smaller amount of stock which is at a higher and higher concentration. You can cook it down quite a bit, since all you're losing is the water; just be sure not to cook it all the way down until it's dry, because you'll ruin your pot and the stock. Just reduce it until it's thicker and darker and lower in the stock pot, but still at least an inch deep in the pot.

When it's cooked down to your liking, allow it to cool and then move it to the refrigerator. Any fat in the stock should rise to the top and form a solid layer that you can just take off once it's cold and solid enough. At this point, depending on how thick your stock is, it may also have solidified due to gelatin in the chicken bones. If that's the case, you may need to warm it a little one final time so that it's a liquid. Then, you can finally pour the stock into ice cube trays to store it indefinitely in the freezer until you need it. How's that for convenient!

When you need it in a recipe, just reconstitute it by adding water. In other words, if the recipe calls for a cup of stock, you can just dissolve a stock cube into a cup of water and use that. You can make it a higher concentration by using two cubes if you want; it will probably taste better but you'll also run out of stock faster. If you made strong, dense stock, you might be able to use a half-cube. It's up to you.

One way to make the straining process a little easier is to use a slotted spoon or strainer to scoop out most of the solids, then reduce it for a little while before you pour it out through a colander to get the rest of the solids—that way you're working with less liquid, which should make it easier.

If that doesn't make any sense, wait until you've done it once, and then read it again.

Another tip: it takes basically the same amount of time to make a large batch of stock as it does to make a small batch, so you might as well make more if you can. Sometimes I'll use as many as three chicken carcasses, 5 or 6 onions, a lot of carrots and celery... you get the picture. If you've got a pot that's big enough, you might as well make more. After all, if you're going to reduce it afterward and freeze it in ice cube trays, storage room won't be an issue.

Homemade stock is extremely delicious and extremely good for you, so give it a shot. It's less difficult than you might think, and it's definitely worth it.

SEASONING

We already touched on this in the "Trial And Error" section, but I wanted to revisit it one more time here at the end.

Obviously, if most people want to stick to any type of eating routine, the food needs to taste good. For some people the basic versions of things we've discussed here will accomplish that—mostly sea salt and black pepper, butter and olive oil, with some wine, stock, or citrus flavors here and there. Honestly, if you can do just those things exactly right, you can make some of the best food anywhere.

However, others will want some more variety or some different flavors. So try some! Pick a seasoning and incorporate it into your next recipe. Just remember these guidelines:

1) Don't experiment with more than one new thing at a time—otherwise, you might not know which new flavor you liked.

2) It's better to use not enough of the new seasoning than it is to use too much. You probably won't like anything if it's overpowering.

You'll develop a sense of how to handle this as you gain experience, but these two tips should cover you until then.

Some of my personal favorite seasonings to work with include:

- sea salt
- black pepper
- garlic powder
- onion powder
- turmeric
- paprika
- cayenne (only use a little! it's hot!)
- chili powder
- cumin
- mustard powder
- garam masala
- wine
- balsamic vinegar
- apple cider vinegar
- stock
- lemon juice

The best way to get confident in the kitchen is to start experimenting with some new flavors. Go for it! You'll be glad you did.

CONNECT WITH ME

For further health, fitness, and nutrition information, you can find me online at BarrettBooks.com. You can read my blog posts and articles, including an ongoing series profiling strongmen, and another featuring common food additives.

You can also get in touch with me directly through the "Contact" page to ask me any exercise or nutrition question you might have, and I'll be happy to answer them as best I can in my "Training Q & A" section, where I answer questions from readers.

You'll see an e-mail sign-up form on the site as well where you can enter your e-mail address to stay up to date on blog posts and new books. You won't get e-mail more than about once a week, and of course I'll never spam you or sell your information, and you can unsubscribe at any time.

Another way to stay up to date is through my Facebook page, which can be found at Facebook.com/BarrettBooks.

One last thing—as I mentioned earlier, reviews on Amazon are a very big deal for authors like me. If you found this book to be helpful, taking a minute to leave a positive review (even a short one) would be enormously appreciated.

I look forward to connecting with you, and please do contact me through my website with any questions or comments you might have.

CONCLUSION

In the modern world, you need to be careful about what you eat and where you eat it. Much of the food that we have access to—especially restaurant food, or prepared foods from other sources—contains preservatives, artificial colorings and flavorings, and a variety of other additives which are put in the food not because they are beneficial to your body, but because they improve the food from a business perspective—longer shelf life, more attractive appearance, and so on.

That means the safest source of food for you and your family is food prepared in your own home, from whole, natural ingredients. That can be a challenge for a lot of people, because you typically can't rely on any of the more convenient options for meals—like frozen or made-for-you foods—and still avoid all those harmful additives.

However, now that you've read this book, you should be in a much better position than most people when facing this problem. You have a better understanding of what exactly you need to avoid in those overly-processed foods, and you know how to find better options.

We talked about the basic tools you'll need to use to avoid frustration and save time in the kitchen, and how to take care of them. We talked about getting fat, protein, and carbohydrates from natural, healthy sources. We covered a list of basic recipes which can be combined and altered to make dozens of different meals, and we talked about how you can find recipes from other sources and modify them to avoid additives. We also talked about the importance of trying out new seasonings and spices so you can discover new flavors, and how to learn how to use them.

All that's left now is for you to start somewhere. Where you need to start will depend on your prior experience and your comfort level in the kitchen, but feel free to pick something extremely simple, like just sautéing vegetables. Use basic seasonings like sea salt and pepper, see how it goes, and make adjustments if you need to for next time.

If you're still getting comfortable with cooking, expect there to be a few nights when dinner doesn't go quite like you thought it would—something might get burned, something might be too salty, some pork or chicken might not be cooked all the way through and need to go back in the pan or the oven. Don't worry about it. It's a learning experience, and you can do better next time.

Many people—even those who consider themselves to be pretty healthy—don't realize the volume of unnatural additives that they put into their bodies on a daily basis. It adds up, and over time it can really be detrimental to your health. The best defense against this problem is a steady dose of meals created in the home. Now you know everything you need to know to make those meals a reality, and to stop the daily influx of harmful additives into your body.

I hope you found this book to be valuable—I sincerely believe that if you put into practice what we've talked about here, it can make a huge, positive difference for your health and well-being. So please, give it a shot. You could be having tastier, healthier, fresher meals, starting tonight.

BOOKS BY PATRICK BARRETT

Natural Exercise: Basic Bodyweight Training And Calisthenics For Strength And Weight-Loss

Advanced Bodyweight Exercises: An Intense Full Body Workout In A Home Or Gym

The Natural Diet: Simple Nutritional Advice For Optimal Health In The Modern World

How To Do A Handstand: From The Basic Exercises To The Free Standing Handstand Pushup

Hand And Forearm Exercises: Grip Strength Workout And Training Routine

Best Ab Exercises: Abdominal Workout Routine For Core Strength And A Flat Stomach

Easy Exercises: Simple Workout Routine For Busy People In The Office, At Home, Or On The Road

One Arm Pull Up: Bodyweight Training And Exercise Program For One Arm Pull Ups And Chin Ups

ABOUT THE AUTHOR

Patrick Barrett has been interested in exercise ever since he started to lift weights with his dad and older brothers as a kid. He participated in a half-dozen organized sports (most notably inline hockey and high school wrestling) until a neck injury during a wrestling match in his junior year prevented him from playing further in any contact sports.

After the injury, he developed an interest in pursuing strength and balance, particularly through bodyweight and self-taught gymnastic-type exercises.

Patrick has always loved both cooking and eating food. Unsatisfied with the confusing and often contradictory nutritional advice offered by mainstream sources, Patrick searched for another way to understand human nutrition that was logical, consistent, and effective. His books on food and nutrition reflect this 'cleaner,' more intuitive and useful understanding of food and how it impacts our health.

Patrick hopes that his books will save his audience time and aggravation by finally offering practical ways to achieve their nutrition and fitness goals.